Encouragement

for the

End Times

DEA A. MYERS

1st Edition

2023

Encouragement for the End Times

Book Title: Never an Accident

1st Edition

Author: Dea A. Myers

Editor: Jessica Hemstreet

ISBN: 978-1-959492-04-7 (Paperback)

ISBN: 978-1-959492-05-4 (Hardcover)

A Dea A. Myers Books and Myers-Hemstreet production.

This book is part of a project of ours called "The Mini Book Project." A project designed for people searching for an objective and meaningful reading.

All Scriptures quoted from NSAB and NIV versions.

Questions and Info: Drop us a line at
deaamyers@gmail.com

Thanks...

To God the Father, You are the One who created and sustains me; To Jesus, You are my savior and my defender, and to the Holy Spirit, I would be lost without Your presence, All the glory to You.

To Jess Hemstreet, my sister in Christ and editor, thank you for running this race with me.

To Pastor Robert Jarrett and Mrs. Beverly Jarrett, thank you for your feedback and input. We praise God for your lives, prayers, and help.

To Chris Myers for his last-minute revision. Thanks for jumping in the boat with us!

To my husband and children, thank you for your love and support.

To my parents, the first ones who taught me about God's love; to all my pastors, my Sunday School Teachers, your loving work was not in vain. Thank you for your dedication.

To all who support our ministry, thank you.

Dea A. Myers

"Strengthen the feeble hands, steady the knees that give way; say to those with fearful hearts, be strong, do not fear, your God will come, He will come with vengeance; with divine retribution. He will come to save you."

Isaiah 35: 3-4.

Encouragement for the End Times

- A Brief Introduction

When we began 2022 Jess, our editor, and I, Dea A. Myers, had a couple of projects in mind to write and edit, but I have to confess- this book wasn't one of them. Everything changed when I felt the Lord compelling me to write about the end times, and here we are releasing this new project called "Encouragement for the End Times".

Since Jesus' ascension, the church awaits for the Lord's return. The apostles were certain Jesus would return in their generation, and the same happened in other times of hardship and pain.

Since the pandemic started in 2020 this world has changed so much, it is hard to believe it is the same world we used to live in three years ago. It all started with the virus. People getting sick, people dying, quarantines, churches replaced their in-person services for online ones. Schools closed, companies closed, political issues, economic crisis, supply issues. The routine of our lives, so familiar to us, was suddenly dissipated, and in the midst of all this, one question popped up: "What if Jesus is coming?" "Are we ready?"

What if this is it? How can we cope emotionally and spiritually with chaos around us? How can we grow in our relationship with Christ? And what tools can we find in the Bible which will help us to deal with the tough times set to arrive?

This book was written to give you some insight into these questions. This inspirational book is divided into blocks of chapters. In each chapter, we will tell you how hard things are predicted to happen, but we will also remind you, you serve a God who fondly loves you and will be with you always till the very end of the age.

Welcome to this journey,

Dea A. Myers.

Coping With Chaos

1. Coping When Love Grows Cold

Love is undoubtedly the force which moves the world. It wakes you up in the middle of the night to check on your children, or what moves you to cook that loved one's special food because you wanted to surprise that special someone. It is also what moved God the Father to send His Son, and what motivated the Son to obey Him; and ultimately, what motivated the Spirit to live in imperfect people like us.

Love is what generates kindness, and kindness is what helps anyone's day to be better, but according to the Bible, the closer we are to Jesus' return, evil will grow, and love will grow cold (Matthew 24:12).

We could mention some examples like the neighbor that won't greet you, the cashier that will treat you badly, or the driver that will cut you off in spite, etc. However, this is only the tip of the iceberg. We are talking about something deeper such as toxic relationships, gossip, judgment, lack of compassion or empathy, and people who take pleasure in hurting others in so many ways.

As shocking as it is to see this happening, this is all predicted in the Bible, in 2 Timothy 3:2-5. Timothy said in the end times, "People will be lovers of themselves, lovers of money, boastful, proud, abusive, disobedient to their parents, ungrateful, unholy," (verse 2). Does this sound familiar to you?

Timothy continues, "...without love, unforgiving, slanderous, without self-control, brutal, not lovers of the good, treacherous, rash, conceited, lovers of pleasure rather than lovers of God..." (2 Timothy 3:3-4).

Can you recognize some of this in our current society? Sadly, I do.

I have always been a type of counselor to my friends and acquaintances, have always listened to their problems and tried to help them, but I am appalled with some of the things I have seen people going through lately. Their circumstances are so surreal they sound like a movie plot. You listen to their stories, and some of the things they go through are so shocking you have difficulty believing they are real, but they're real. That person is really going through this. It is shocking, but real.

The text continues and Timothy says, "...having a form of godliness but denying its power," (2 Timothy 3:5). Do you know what that means? It means some of these people seem to be good people, some of them may even go to church. They dress like the people of the church, they talk like them, but they have not surrendered their hearts to Jesus. They deny the Lord's power because they never allowed the Lord to transform them.

You may say, "I know I am a sinner, but I am not this person. I am a person who prays for others, who feels others' pains, who truly seeks the Lord." And I praise the Lord because there are still many people like you, but the challenge is, how are you going to deal with the other people, those Timothy mentions?

We all know Jesus wants us to love our neighbors, but how are we going to deal with abusive people? How are we going to continue loving people and manage to live well around them? What kind of advice would the Bible have for us in this particular situation?

Do you know what Proverbs 4:23 says? It says we need to guard our hearts because our life (and consequently, our acts and words), come from it. If we want our acts and words to honor the Lord, we definitely need to protect our hearts to some extent.

What about Timothy? What does he say about those selfish, ungrateful, unkind people? Surprisingly he says, "Have nothing to do with these people," (2 Timothy 3:5). The advice seems selfish and harsh, but ultimately, his advice places, first and foremost, the kingdom of God. Timothy knows disruptive relationships usually take away one's energy, strength, emotional, spiritual, and mental balance. It is very important to note He doesn't tell you to stop praying for them, or to stop blessing them or stop loving them, but clearly, he believes we need to be prudent concerning our relationships.

Jesus says in Matthew 22:36 we need to love our neighbor as we love ourselves. It means you cannot love others in a balanced way if you don't love yourself. We need to be well in order to love others in a productive and healthy way. In other words, we need to keep sane and emotionally healthy so we can serve the Lord and others in a positive way.

The love of many will grow cold in the last days, but Jesus is still calling us to continue loving others. He is calling us to keep seeking Him, loving Him with all our hearts, and allowing the Spirit to fill us so we can continue loving others.

Loving our neighbor was challenging in the past, and it is even more so now, but Jesus still wants us to do it at the same time we manage to protect our own hearts and souls. He told us to stand firm and if we do this, we will be saved (Mathew 24:12-13). So, stand firm in His love, love others, and protect your heart.

2. Coping with the Growth of Wickedness

The Bible says evil will grow in the last days. The closer we are to the Lord's return, the more evil will spread on Earth. The Lord will allow evildoers to prosper and iniquity to grow, and sometimes, prevail. As we serve a just and fair God, we have this inner desire for justice. We want to see justice happen, but at the end times, this dynamic will change, and this is going to be heart wrenching to watch.

I am not saying there has never been injustice because we know this has not been the case, but in the last days, people will change, society will change, values will change and the closer we are to Jesus' return, evil will become more and more oppressive and prominent.

We are going to see the liars, corrupt people and deceivers prevailing. They will lie and deceive in broad daylight, and you will think, "They will not escape from justice," but they will. It will seem that nothing or no one will have the power to stop them. And it will be hard to live in a place like this. You may feel like God is not seeing what is going on, you may feel abandoned by God, but Jesus told us in Luke 21:9 to not be frightened, because it would be necessary for these things to happen.

And one could ask why God would allow those things to happen? I think what God is doing is giving us a huge amount of freedom to see who we really are inside. Think about this, if we live in a relatively just place, where laws are upheld and evil does not prevail, this will hold us back from doing any wrong thing. As an example, we will never rob a store if we know we will go to jail, right?

But what if all the people who did such things found a way to do it without getting arrested? How many more of them would do it? And I am talking in all spheres of society- moral, political, economic, and spiritual... God is giving us freedom to see how true our commitment to Him is. He wants to see who we really are.

And while we are going through this, while many of us will use our last breath to honor the Lord, others won't. They will go in the opposite direction, and evil will spread throughout the Earth in a way never seen before.

Keeping the faith in a time like this is not going to be easy. Sometimes we will just need a moment to let these things sink in. We will need a moment of quietness to process what has just happened right before our eyes until we are able to keep going. We may even need some time to cry before the Lord, or cry out to him, or ask for His help or comfort and direction because we will be surrounded by trials and hardships.

But after we cry, after we are shocked and frustrated, we will need to remember the words of Jesus saying to not be discouraged, because it is necessary for those things to happen. We will need to remember God has control over everything.

We will need to keep in mind, as much as He will give authority for evil to spread, *His Spirit* will continue to act in a *powerful way.* God is still our Father, and the Holy Spirit is still with us, and Jesus said He would be with us until the end of the age. He will not abandon us. We sometimes promise things we won't fulfill, but Jesus always fulfills each one of His promises.

On a side note, if you read the Bible, you know what is going to happen in the end. According to the Bible, Jesus is coming the second time to judge the earth. In the right time, divine justice will happen. In the right time, according to the Bible, good will prevail. So, keep the faith. Even if trials happen, you won't be alone. He will be with you until the end.

3. Coping with Changes

Human beings love to be in control. I mean, we love to think we are in control. Honestly, we have never been in control, but we like the feeling or the idea of it. We like to sit at the table, grab our notepads and establish our goals for short, middle and long-term periods. Then, life comes and, BAM, everything changes.

How many people had to cancel their plans during the pandemic? How many trips, flights, ceremonies and gatherings had to be canceled or postponed? Many, right? I guess the majority of us had to deal with frustration of seeing our plans being cancelled, altered or postponed.

Truth is, our fight for control started in the garden. The desire to know good and evil, to be like God was in fact an attempt to be in control. But we aren't in control, and it really bothers us. It was like this in the past, it has been like this since the pandemic, and the closer we are to the Lord's return, this feeling of insecurity will grow even more. The more we have to deal with unseen and unexpected situations, this instability may push you to a state of anxiety, panic attacks, etc.

In Brazil, we have something called "Yellow September." It is a month of awareness, and it aims to prevent suicide and motivate people to seek help in case of need.

A friend of mine, who is a teacher in Brazil was talking about suicide with her teenager students in September 2021. She started the conversation asking how many of them had ever thought about taking their own lives. She was heartbroken when 70 percent of the class raised their hands. Shocking, isn't it? Absolutely.

This feeling of uncertainty and instability can spiral our emotions, our spirituality, and it may crush our faith and hope for the future. How can we deal with this? First of all, we need to learn to be more flexible. We need to understand some of our plans will happen, some will not, and some may happen in a different way or time than we expected.

I know it is hard, but we need to understand we can't control life. God is the boss. He is the one in control and He knows what is best for us. So, keep planning, dreaming, and establishing goals, but ultimately, we need to understand God's will is going to prevail.

There are two people in this world who know you very well. The first one is God Himself. Nobody in this world knows you more than He does. The Holy Spirit lives in your heart and is able to clearly identify your feelings and thoughts. So, if you can't identify what is going on with you – pray and ask God to show you what is going on, what is making your emotions worse, ask for healing and direction on how to deal with them.

I never had to pray for emotions in my lifetime but after the pandemic I started to do so. And I do the same for my friends. Many times when I ask them how I can pray for them, the answer is the same - emotions. So, don't be afraid to pray, to ask God to show you what is going on in your heart, how to deal with your feelings, etc.

The second person who knows you very well is yourself. Not even your mother knows you better than yourself. You have walked in your shoes for some time now, and at this point, you know a lot about yourself. You know your limits, you know when you are about to break, and bottom line, you know when you are not "okay."

The problem is we are in a society which tells you, you can't stop. You know you are not okay, but the mentality of "You got to push through" (like it doesn't matter what happens, you can't stop) does not allow you to do so. You feel guilty, feel lazy or selfish if you take some time for yourself or to preserve yourself. But the truth is the philosophy of "you got to push through" has its limits, and if you push it too hard, it may lead you to an emotional, spiritual and mental state that is not good.

God created the world in six days and rested on the seventh. Jesus said in the Bible this resting day was not created because of God, but because of us. God doesn't need to rest. We do. We all need a day to rest, take a decent nap, and put our minds in order. This time of quietness is important for us to decompress.

If you are a person whom people seek for counseling and advice, such as a pastor, a leader, a counselor, or simply a friend people seek in times of need, you will probably need to take a break once in a while too. One cannot carry all the emotional weight of the world. The only one who could, did and does is Jesus.

Since 2020, bad news seems to pile up day-after-day and we need to understand we are limited human beings who can only take so much at a time. The closer it is to Jesus' return, the more we will have to deal with changes, calamities, bad news and things never seen before. You will need to take care of your mind and heart. So, if you need to be off for some time, do it. As we said before, we need to be well to be able to offer support to others.

Speaking of decompressing, what are the things which could help you when you feel overwhelmed? Reading the Word of God surely is one of the first things. Praying to God leads us to ask for help from the One who can relieve our hearts from the burdens of this world. Worship also reminds us of the promises of God and leads us to glorify Him, declaring our trust in Him.

And what about on an earthly level, what could help you to decompress? A time off social media and tv news? Having some time for some physical activities? Keeping yourself busy will help you when your mind is overwhelmed. Seeking a moment of quietness in the backyard, or having some coffee with a friend, even if it is only a phone call, reading a nice book, or watching a good and positive movie might help.

Know, above all else, you are not alone. You are not the only one going through this. We all are. If you think you need help, ask for it, don't hesitate.

All these things mentioned above can help us to deal with the bad days, but none of them can ever replace what we can find in the Lord. The promises available in the Scriptures give us hope in the darkest days, and so does worship and prayer. So hang on onto this hope and take care of your emotions in order to fulfill God's plans for you in His kingdom.

Glory and Power

Jesus Glorified

When you think about Jesus, what image pops up in your mind? Jesus walking among men? Jesus resurrected? Jesus crucified? The most popular image of Christ, apart from the nativity, is the crucifixion. The image of the Son of God hanging on a cross, paying for our imperfection, sins and flaws.

The image of His supreme sacrifice is so strong that it sticks with us. For some people, He is still hanging on that cross. For some people, He is still there. But let me remind you, He is not. The cross of Christ was the most important chapter of human history according to the Bible, but it was one chapter in Jesus' glorious story.

What happened with Jesus after the cross? The resurrection, then after 40 days, He ascended to Heaven. But what happened with Jesus after that? What does He look like? What happens in Heaven when Jesus is around? Revelation is rich in information about Jesus' glory.

It is valuable and extremely important to have this new perspective about Jesus. At the end times, or during the process of it, as we said previously, things are going to get hard, and we are going to have that feeling that evil is overcoming good, as we have seen in the previous chapter.

We will have tough days and we will need hope. We are going to need to feed our minds with things which will give us strength to continue, instead of discouragement. And in those days, we are going to need to keep in mind who the Savior we serve truly is. Do you know the Jesus you serve? Let me tell you who He is.

Revelation was written by Jesus' apostle named John. Because of his faith in Jesus, John was exiled to the Island of Patmos, and while he was there, away from everything, the Lord gave Him a vision, and told him to write in a book what he was seeing.

John wrote he listened to a voice and when he turned to see who was talking to Him, he saw

Jesus. He described to us what He was like. Jesus was like a Son of Man. He was dressed in a robe with a golden sash on His chest. His hair was white like wool and His eyes were like blazing fire. His feet were glowing, and His voice was like the sound of rushing waters. His face was like the sun shining in all its brilliance. (Rev. 1:12-16)

The Jesus who once left His throne in Heavens to be confined in a human body, the same Jesus who bore our trespasses on the cross and resurrected three days later, now shines before John in all His glory.

John was probably in awe and so afraid of His glory that he fell on his face. Jesus placed His right hand on John and told him not to be afraid. In the Bible, Jesus told John He Himself is the first and the last, the Living One, the One who was dead and is now alive forever.

In chapter 5:2-5 of Revelation, John describes a scroll which needed to be opened but no one had authority to open the scroll. John cried because nobody could break the seals and open the scroll. Jesus, the lamb of God, was the only one who had authority to break the seals to open it. He, together with His Father, is worshiped in Heaven by all creatures and angels.

In Revelation 19:11, Jesus is described as the Heavenly Warrior, riding a white horse. He is called Faithful and True. He is the one who will bring justice to earth. On His robe and on His thigh is written, "KINGS OF KINGS AND LORD OF THE LORDS."

Jesus tells John more about Himself in the first four chapters. He is the one who holds the keys of death and hades, and He is the one who has the key of David, which can open any door. Do you know what that means? Jesus has authority over death, even over hell. He has the key of David, which means He has the authority to open and close any door. There is nothing you can ask Him that is impossible for Him. He can open any door, answer any prayer, and fulfill any desire of our hearts.

Yes. This is the Jesus you serve. The One who is seated at the right of God the Father. The Magnificent One, with eyes blazing like fire, whose face shines. The One that is praised and worshiped and glorified. The One who has authority to do things none of us could ever imagine, worthy of our worship, commitment, and love.

The Power of Jesus

The Bible tells us in Luke 21: 9–11 in the last days there will be wars and rumors of wars, earthquakes, pestilences, famines, and signs from the heavens. And if the Bible says, it is going to happen. Day- after-day we will have to deal with bad news. It is going to be hard, and in the midst of it all, we may feel discouraged and think nothing good will happen anymore.

This kind of feeling or train of thought may drag our faith down, and ultimately is not a good way to perceive things. YES, we will be surrounded by negative news, surrounded by devastating changes in society, and we will be dealing with grievance and pain, but God will still be with us, helping us in all sorts of ways.

The last days will not change God's nature. He will be the same God. According to Hebrews 13:8, "Jesus Christ is the same yesterday and today and forever." No matter what period of human history we are in, He still loves us, and, in one way or another, He will provide.

In those days, we will need to remember Jesus has the key of David who opens and closes any door and has enough power to help us and bless us in any way.

The Gospels are full of demonstrations of Jesus' power. While in this world, Jesus raised people from the dead, healed all types of disease, blessed fishermen with a net full of fish even after an unfruitful night of effort and work. He did the impossible. He changed lives, hearts and rescued souls.

It doesn't matter what times we are living in, God has the power to feed you in the middle of a famine, to give you prosperity in the middle of an economic crisis, to heal you from all diseases, and even raise you from the dead, or give you peace in the middle of the chaos.

The closer we are to Jesus' return, *we will need to remember this*. We serve a powerful God who loves us and will never abandon us or stop caring for our needs. If we focus on the bad things which are happening in this world, our negative emotions will drag our faith to the ground. And I don't know about you, but I do believe if our faith is on the ground it is going to be hard to stand up.

Do whatever you have to do to feed your faith. Read the word, worship God, pray at all times, and seek for every possible thing that helps you feed your faith. There are numerous sermons on the internet. Each one of us identifies more with some preachers than others. We can listen to a sermon per day, or twice a week for encouragement, write verses of the Bible which are going to remind you of who God is. Place them on the fridge or in front of your desk at work but DO it. We need to focus on God's promises in the tough times.

As we said before, Jesus is good, that's His nature. It is not Dea A. Myers who is telling you this. It is the Word of God. Hold onto this Word. He will always find a way to help us and bless us even in the middle of chaos. Do your part. Seek for things which will strengthen your faith as He will remain faithful to His promises.

Seven Promises for Seven Churches

Seven Promises for Seven Churches

For years, I avoided reading the book of Revelation and continued to do so, until one day I felt it was time to read it. When I opened the book, I read all those things I was afraid of all the calamities set to happen in the tribulation times. But I also found more than this. There are promises hidden in all parts of this book. Those promises gave me hope and that's why I decided to dedicate a whole section of this book to the promises God has for the seven churches.

First of all, who were the seven churches? The seven churches described in Revelation referred to churches from the time the book was written. But not coincidentally, this text still can be used in our modern churches and in our spiritual lives. Because churches are more than buildings, they are made of people like you and me. People with virtues and failures, and God had promises for each one of them.

There is a lot to learn from each church. Some of their weaknesses will be very similar to our own, but the same way the Lord had promises for those churches who kept faithful to him until the end, He has promises for us.

One of the things I absolutely love in these letters is their order. Do you know the very first thing that happens in each letter? Jesus commends them for their good deeds. Can you imagine this? The Son of God, The King of Kings, The One who is glorified in Heaven sees your works and recognizes them.

How amazing is this? Do you remember the day you went to bed late after serving Jesus at the church? Or the day you were offered to do something illegal, and you refused to do it? Or the day you honored Him following His Word? Those little acts nobody saw, but God did, and those letters are the proof of it.

The second thing in those letters is Jesus tells them about their flaws, temptations, or weaknesses, and what He sees in that particular church. He says, "I have this against you." This is not because He was angry, or because He was putting them down, but He knew they needed to improve, and grow. He is telling each church what areas they need to repent, improve and what they need to do to fix it. In the same way, we need those admonitions and reminders.

This is Him taking care of each church individually and personally as He does with each one of us. Fixing what needs to be fixed is important for our sanctification, and for us to be closer and closer to God.

At the end after exposing their weaknesses, He says those who are faithful to Him to the end will be rewarded with a special and unique reward for each one of the churches. So let's see what we can learn from each church.

1. Ephesus

In the letter to the church of Ephesus, Jesus commends the church for their dedication. He says He knows their deeds, their hard work, their perseverance, and the way they have dealt with false apostles. He also commends them for the way they have persevered and endured hardships for His name and managed, despite the hardships, to not get discouraged.

The Ephesians' virtues were admirable. They were absolutely a hard-working church, but He said He had something against them. They had forgotten the love they had at first.

Sad, isn't it? This diligent church was so hardworking and zealous, but they no longer had the love they had in the beginning towards the Lord. I'd guess some of us share this problem. We can check the boxes - get early to the service, work in church events, and tithe to the Lord, but deep inside our love for the Lord is not the same anymore.

Sometimes we see people who are so indifferent concerning many things around them, completely change when talking about something they are passionate about. Their eyes sparkle and their faces beam when they talk about sports, movies, music, cars, family members, travels, possessions and so on... But the same sparkle is not there when they talk about Jesus.

This is what Jesus is talking about. Like He says in Matthew 6:21, "For where your treasure is, there your heart will be also." Jesus knew the church was committed to Him, but the sparkle was gone, and He wanted them to be passionate about the gospel again. Jesus tells them to repent and to change their ways as He tells them to listen to the Spirit and leaves them a promise. To the victorious one, He would give the right to eat from the tree of life located in God's paradise.

We used to have access to this tree in the Garden, but because of our disobedience, we've lost access to all the blessings the garden had to offer. He promised if they remained faithful, they would have the right to eat that fruit again. It is a promise from Christ.

2. The Smyrna Church

Jesus begins the letter saying He knows about their poverty and afflictions, but He says they are in fact rich. This church was being slandered. Some religious people were making false statements about them, ruining their reputation.

Jesus said those slanderers were in fact being used by the enemy.

He knew exactly what the church of Smyrna was going through and also the things they were about to suffer – imprisonment and persecution for ten days.

Jesus tells them in this letter to be faithful until the end and He Himself would give them their life as a "victor crown." He tells them to listen to the Spirit and they would not experience the second death, which is the eternal death.

The church of Smyrna was going through a very difficult time. They were not only facing poverty, living in a difficult situation, but also were facing false accusations. I bet some of us know how hard this is. Especially after the social media era, it has become so easy for a person to destroy someone's work or reputation with a tap of a keyboard. Sometimes you want to defend yourself, but you feel you don't have a voice. The church found themselves in this position. They didn't have money, status, or influential members, and they didn't have anyone to defend them.

Many times when facing situations like these, we feel powerless, we feel our lack of money or prestige may put us in a more vulnerable position. But you know what? Jesus sees it all. He sees everything that is going on. He knows who you really are, and at the right time, He will reward you for your commitment to Him. For those approved by the Lord, Jesus promises them they will not face eternal death.

3. The Pergamum Church

Wow! As soon as we start to read this portion of scripture, I think of how hard it is to imagine what this church was going through. Jesus says Satan has his throne in this city. In other words, Satan lived in this city. Would you like to live in a place like that?

A city where Satan lives is a city which is corrupted in all sorts of ways. A place where you may witness all sorts of injustices, lies, deceit, bribery, greed, immorality and spiritual decay. The Bible says you cannot serve God and the enemy at the same time, and this is true.

When we live in a place influenced by God's values, the city has a good atmosphere. The Spirit flows and bears fruit in the place. There is peace, there is joy, there is faith and there is hope, even in tough and challenging circumstances. But when it is the opposite and people start to seek more for the enemy's values than God's, the Holy Spirit doesn't flow in the place as He used to. It is the enemy who takes over and instead of peace, there is anguish; instead of faith, there is fear; instead of joy, there is sadness and lastly, instead of hope, there is discouragement.

Have you been to a place like this? I have, and let me tell you, it is hard. You feel like there is a black cloud on top of the city. You feel there is something trying to put you down. Your spirit conflicts with the spirit which is ruling the place, which may lead to something known as spiritual oppression.

Living in a city like this, while serving God Almighty it is not easy. It is a constant spiritual battle to do what you would easily do elsewhere and a constant battle to be positive, hopeful and cheerful.

Well, this is the place where the church of Pergamum was located. Jesus knew how hard it was for them to live and continue to serve Him in that atmosphere. He commends them for not renouncing and for remaining true to His name, even in the days when there was an atmosphere of persecution and fear. Even after Antipas (Jesus' faithful servant) was put to death, which caused them to fear for their own lives, they continued to serve Jesus.

The problem of living in a place like this is, it is hard to keep the church pure, without worldly influences. You are living in that atmosphere, and it is easy for heresies to invade the church. This is exactly what Jesus charged them.

This church, which managed to survive in spite of living in a dreadful atmosphere, had some people who taught them things the Lord absolutely detested. They would sacrifice food to idols, eat the food and commit sexual immorality. They also had people in the church who held the teachings of the Nicolaitans, which the Lord also disapproved of. As hard as it is to believe, this was going on in the church.

This is also a lesson for us today. People talk about God in a way as if He has changed, but He hasn't. He is the only absolute constant thing this world has ever had. The Bible says the Lord doesn't change. So if it was wrong in the past, it is now. This is why it is so vital for us to know the Word of God.

I was reading in Proverbs the other day about six things the Lord hates (Proverbs 6:16-19), and let me tell you, our society is full of it. At some point, in our journey as Christians, we stopped reading the Bible, and consequently, we've ended up letting the world's values get inside our churches, and ultimately, our hearts. The same way Jesus tells the church of Pergamum to deal with the wrong teachings, He expects us to do the same.

On a side note, to the church of Pergamum, Jesus promised two rewards for the faithful ones. They would eat from the hidden manna and receive a white stone with a new name.

The manna was the food God provided to the Israelites when they were in the desert. It was the food which came from the heavens to His people.

It tasted like nothing else we have ever produced in this world and was sweet as honey.

There are a lot of interpretations for the expression hidden manna. The most common ones are that God has withheld the manna Himself since it couldn't be found anymore in this world. He is saving it for all His believers to taste it in the New Jerusalem. Others believe Jesus is the hidden manna Himself since Jesus in John 6:51 refers to Himself as "the living bread that came down from heaven and whoever eats from it will live forever." So, that would be a clear reference about Eternal Life.

Among all the interpretations, as there are many, one thing is sure - God was the Israelites' provider in the desert, such as Jesus was the provider of a hungry crowd who were listening to His sermons. And the idea is God the Father, and the Son will do the same in their Kingdom. They will be our main provider.

There are also theories about the white stone. One of the most common ones is that the white stone represents purity. The same way Abraham, Jacob and Paul had their names changed by the

Lord; we will receive a new name given by the Lord Himself.

4. The Thyatira Church

Jesus starts His letter to the church of Thyatira saying He knows their deeds, love, faith, service, and perseverance. He sees their progress, along with how they were doing more for the kingdom than before. Again, this touches me every time Jesus sees each one of their acts of love towards Him.

But this church was also going through serious issues spiritually. They allowed a woman, who entitled herself a prophet, to teach, but in fact her teachings were leading people to sin against the Lord.

She was not only leading people to practice immorality, but practicing immorality with them, and was also leading people to eat food sacrificed to idols. The Lord was compassionate and gave her time to repent, but she refused. So the Lord announced judgment would come to her, her house and those who partook with her in such acts.

But the Lord still loved the Thyatira church and said everyone who hadn't partaken of her teachings would not be disciplined. To the victorious, Jesus promised authority over the nations and the morning star, which according to Revelation 22:16 is Jesus Himself. He is our inheritance, the Light of the World and the One who brightens our days.

5. The Sardis Church

The letter to the church of Sardis is not an easy one, but at the same time this church can teach us a very important lesson. This church had a reputation of being spiritually alive, but they were not. Jesus said they were dead spiritually, commanded them to wake up, to repent, and to strengthen their path, which touches my heart a lot.

Why? Because as humans, we have the tendency to see the outside and to be led by appearances or looks. From a human perspective, this church was vibrant, active and alive, but in fact, it was spiritually dead. It was far from God and His principles, which is not impossible to happen in our time. The church was more focused on pleasing men than God. It became more of a social club than the house of the Lord. They cared more about what men thought about them than the Lord Himself. A church lacking the most important element, of a true and deep relationship with the Lord.

Churches are made of people like you and me, and we may deal with the same issue in our lives. It is easy to get used to going to church every Sunday, but are our hearts alive before the Lord? Do we really love the Lord and His principles, or are we going to church out of habit or tradition or to have social interaction? If that's your case, there is still time to fix the situation. Jesus still loves you and misses you opening your heart to him. If you are breathing, there is still time to develop a real, deep and meaningful relationship with the Lord.

Regarding the church of Sardis, Jesus promises to those who "hadn't soil their clothing," they will be dressed in white, which means they will be pure, will have their names in the Book of Life and have their names acknowledged before His Father and His angels.

6. The Philadelphia Church

The letter to the Philadelphia church absolutely touches my heart. In this letter, Jesus says that the church has little strength, however, they haven't denied His name and have kept His word. I love when Jesus says they have little strength because many times we feel like this. Many times we feel weak and powerless, but the power of God in us helps us to keep going, to keep honoring Jesus' name and to keep His Word in our hearts.

Like the church of Smyrna, they were also facing false accusations, but they patiently endured the hard times. Jesus tells them their persecutors would recognize He loved the Philadelphia church and promised them they would escape from the hour of trial.

Jesus also tells them He is coming soon and advises them to keep committed to Him so they would not lose their crown. He makes some beautiful promises to those who will stay faithful. Jesus says He will build a pillar in the temple of God (everlasting, durable construction) and promises them they will never leave that place. This means the alliance He has with them in His kingdom will last forever.

To ratify this alliance, He will write on them His new name.

7. The Laodicea Church

The letter written to the Laodicea church is not an easy one either. But as it was with the church of Sardis, this letter has a lot to teach us. Jesus says He knows their deeds as they are not hot or cold but in fact, they are lukewarm. The same way we can't stand to have lukewarm water in our mouths and want to spit it out, Jesus wanted to do the same with this church.

When we think about the word lukewarm, not hot or cold, some people could be led to think about balance, but in this case, I don't think about balance, I think about indifference. Those people's trust and faith were not in the Lord, but in their possessions, accomplishments, and their self-sufficiency.

Self-sufficiency is something very dangerous since it causes us to think we don't need anything or anyone because of our human accomplishments and financial stability. Jesus exposed this weakness of the Laodicean church. He told them to repent and to seek in Him all they needed.

Upon this charge, He promised them if they did this, and if they succeeded in the task of relying solely on Him, they would have the right to sit on His throne. James 4:10 says if we humble ourselves before the Lord, He will lift us up.

When I read about this church, I relate to how we are living our lives today by putting our assurance in the money we have in the bank, instead of the Lord. And those things give us a false sense of security, but that's all they are. What if the stock market crashes in a couple of weeks? All your investments will be gone. What if you get sick? Remember the last pandemic? Everything changed in the blink of an eye. The security this world offers us is temporary or non-existent, but the security we have in Jesus lasts forever.

A Letter to you

We have navigated in this chapter through the seven churches. We saw their deeds and what Jesus commended them for. We saw their flaws, the things they had to do to improve, and the beautiful and unique promises the Lord had for each one of them.

If Jesus wrote you a letter today, what would He commend you for? What are the things you have done so far for Him and His kingdom? It is so important you ask yourself these questions because your honest answers will paint a picture of your level of commitment to Christ. And while your answers may lead you to realize how hard you have worked for the kingdom, they also may lead you in the opposite direction. You may realize you have been so involved with this world, even in your free time, you have done very little for the kingdom.

It is hard to change a situation if we don't ask ourselves these hard questions. The good news is God gave gifts to each one of us. There is not a single "ungifted" child of God in this world. The good news is it doesn't matter how busy you are, there will always be a little bit of free time left, so you can use it to serve God and people. Other good news is there are a million ways we can serve others and, most importantly, it is never too late to start doing it.

Going to the next section of the letter, what would be your flaws as a Christian? What are the things you need to repent of and change? Sometimes it is hard, even for ourselves, to answer this question in an accurate way. But if this is not clear to you, you can ask God, like David asked in Psalm 139:23-24, "Search me, God, and know my heart; put me to test and know my anxious thoughts; and see if there is any hurtful way in me and lead me in the everlasting way." Ask God about it. Having this answer is a good starting point. Allowing the Holy Spirit to make the changes you need is the next step.

And at that point you may ask, what about the promises Jesus has in store for us? Researchers estimate there are at least 3.000 promises from God the Father, Jesus and the Holy Spirit to us. At least! All these promises are made by a God, who never changes and fulfills His promises at the right time.

Jeremiah 29:11 says, "For I know the thoughts I think toward you, says the Lord, thoughts of peace and not evil, to give you a future and hope."

So, keep going. Commit to His kingdom, allow the Spirit to change your heart and hang onto His promises.

Spiritual Tools for the End Times

1. Prayers at the Altar

This next block of chapters we will be talking about the tools we can find in Christianity to help us during a difficult time.

As a Christian, there are some topics, stories or ministries which fascinate me. Prayer is one of them. I love to get my "My Prayer Requests Book," and pray over the requests in it. In the past, prayer was my last resource, but today it is my first response to any problems or issues in my life.

Jesus says in Matthew 11:28, "Come to Me, all who are weary and burdened, and I will give you rest." After three years of having a prayer routine, I can tell you I do believe in it 100%. Many times when I start to pray, I am heavy and burdened, but the more I pray for something or someone, the lighter I feel.

This really touches my heart because Jesus is literally telling you to put your burdens on Him, He will not only carry your burdens, but He will alleviate your heart. I can tell you by experience, this is true in my life.

Why is prayer so important? Prayer is the channel we have to communicate with God. It is how we open our hearts to the Lord and share with Him our needs, dreams, and what is happening in our daily lives. It is also a tool in which we can manifest our love for Him.

The closer we are to Jesus' return the tougher things are going to get. The end times are going to be difficult. We are talking about all the elements going absolutely out of place and order. Jesus said the seas will roar, and if He said so, I do believe it will happen, among other things. Evil will be spreading everywhere, love will grow cold, there will be famines, shortages, pestilences, deaths, wars, and to survive it all, we will need to pray as we never have before.

The Bible also teaches us to pray in Jesus' name (John 14:13). When we are praying in Jesus' name, we are connecting Earth to Heavens by the authority of Jesus. Yes, we are talking about the same Jesus, who has authority to change every situation, even death. If we want to see something happening on Earth, it needs to reach Heavens first, because it is from Heavens which comes God's blessings upon Earth.

Then you may ask, "What are the things I should pray for regarding the end times?" On a personal level, you can pray for protection, provision, guidance and spiritual discernment. As a servant of God you can pray to continue being faithful to Him, to have opportunities to serve Him and sharing His love with others.

Jesus said it would be necessary for those horrid things to happen, but with so many things happening around us, discouragement may lead us away from prayer, thinking God has forgotten us or doesn't listen to our prayers anymore.

But Scriptures say this is far from the truth. God cares for every sincere request which comes from your heart. Revelation 5:8 says the 24 elders and the four living creatures worshiped Jesus in Heaven and each one of them were holding golden bowls of incense, which are the prayers of God's people.

Isn't it amazing? God didn't discard your prayers and threw them in a bin. Instead, your request became incense in God's presence. God cares about each one of our requests. He does. Ultimately as a father, He wants to do what is best for us and for His kingdom, even when we can't understand. The last days will be tough, and some of our requests will be denied. That's true, but we can't give up on prayer, because while some will be denied, others will become reality.

Whatever happens, we must continue to pray. For our sanity, for our spiritual life, for our connection with our Father because Jesus Himself said in Luke 21:35-36 that chaos would come over all at the end times. But He also said, "Pray that you can escape all these things that are about to happen." So Jesus is telling you trials will come to all, but at the same time He is telling us to pray to escape those things. Even at the end times, our prayers will be heard.

So, don't give up! Keep praying. Keep praying with the sincerity of your heart. Your prayers will reach God's throne.

2. Watch the Signs

The first thing you need to know is Jesus wanted to share the signs of the end times with us. He did this in Luke 21 and Mathew 24. He was very clear in Revelation 1:1. God wants to prepare us for what is going to take place, He doesn't want to catch us by surprise because He cares about us. He doesn't want us to be desperate or feel abandoned. He wants to share His plan with us so we will know everything is going according to His will and plan.

I have always loved the Bible, always! I have always loved reading the Bible, New and Old Testament, well, with one exception: The Book of Revelation. Yes, as I said before, I was that type of Christian who read everything, but skipped Revelation. Why? I had a little bit of panic about the book. This is one of the reasons I think writing this book is so important to me. It is an opportunity to show people how accessible this book really is.

I was afraid of the book because everything seemed so enigmatic, so much written in figurative languages, so many allegories, and the news was, wow, tough to swallow. I felt like a housewife who cleans the whole house, but that little corner, close to the bookcase. The day had come I knew I had to face the fear. And I did it. Maybe you are not identifying with this story, but I am sure some are. I was in my mid-thirties when I read for the first time the book of Revelation.

So, when I opened the book, I realized many things. One of them there were so many details about Heaven, about Jesus, God the Father, the angels, and the Heavenly creatures I didn't know about, and they were all there. I was always so eager to learn more about Jesus and His Father. So for me it was absolutely interesting. Second, yeah, I was right about the bad news, but third, there were so many promises of Jesus to us it really touched my heart.

A friend of mine recently asked my opinion about it. She said she was going to purchase several books about Revelation and asked my opinion about it and I was absolutely opposed to it. Why is that? Because the Christian community is extremely diverse, with different doctrines and perceptions. To be honest, sometimes I think each author, pastor, or leader has their own version of how the events of the end times are going to unfold. They are so different she would probably get more confused by reading all those books.

I advised her to read the Bible itself. We do have the Holy Spirit and the Holy Spirit is our teacher. He is, in fact, eager to show us and teach us about Jesus.

Reading "Revelation" is like studying a foreign language. When you start to read the book, everything looks so strange, different, and hard to understand. It is hard not to feel overwhelmed with it. But as I said, it is like learning a language. The more you listen to that language, the more you get familiar with it, the more things start to become clear to you.

For example, the first time I read about Jesus' appearance in Revelation, it really shocked me. I was used to Jesus' earthly appearance, at least how He was presented in movies, tv series, paintings, etc. But with time, I became used to it. According to Revelation, Jesus' hair is white, His eyes are like fire, and His face shines. Today, His image is beautiful and somewhat known to my mind.

The more you read, things are going to get clearer and are going to settle in your brain. People think Revelation has a lot of figurative language, and it has some, but today I think many things are also literal in the book. What happens is since we haven't seen many of these signs, we have the tendency to believe they are not literal.

Take the example of Noah. Noah tried to tell people over and over again they had to repent from their wicked ways because the Lord was going to send water from the skies, and many would die. Many didn't believe in Noah because until that point it hadn't rained on earth, so in their minds it would never happen. But when the first drops of rain started to fall from the skies, I am sure they believed Noah was right.

Yes, there is some figurative language. For example, I am sure many of us do not believe the

Beast is a real beast like a dragon, right? It may be a system of a government, or an oppressive movement, or a leader who will bring tyrannical control and oppression to the world. So, yeah, Revelation has its figurative language, I am not saying otherwise, but I do believe many of the things described in this book are literal.

When we say *literal,* we need to understand John was simply writing what he was seeing. For example, John says he saw a moon which looked covered in blood. But have you heard about a phenomenon called "Bloody Moon?" It just happened in November of 2022. The moon gets red exactly as it was described in Revelation. It wasn't covered in blood, but it looked like it, exactly like John saw it.

So, for us to prepare for the last days, it is extremely important to read the texts about the end times in the Bible. You won't recognize the signs if you don't know what the signs are. So, we need to read the Scriptures and keep our eyes open to what is happening around us.

After you read these scriptures one or two times, I would recommend you start reading other books about the theme and see for yourself what makes sense. It is important to be open and to respect differences because it is common for someone you love in the church to have a very different perspective about the book and its prophecies.

Maybe you are interested in what I am saying now, but you are confused about it. Where can you start? Well, one of the things you could do is search on the web for verses of the Bible about the end times. Research, write down the verses and read them. So, this will start to build in your heart a foundation about the theme.

Besides, there are well-known texts about the end times which will be a great beginning for you. Some of these are Matthew 24, Luke 21, the book of Revelation, and some chapters of the book of Daniel. The rest of the references you can find on the web and keep going from there.

It is time to build your own foundation about the end times. Write the signs down and watch for them. At some point, they will happen. Jesus said in Luke 21: 33, Heaven and Earth would pass, but His words will never pass away. Research. Read. Study. Recognize the signs.

3. Listen to the Spirit

One of the most common sentences of the book of Revelation is, "Listen to what the Spirit says to the church." Jesus says this over and over again throughout this book. If you are thinking why, the answer can be found in Luke 21 of how the Spirit plays a big role in the end of the times.

Let's talk a little bit about the Holy Spirit. First of all, let me tell you something, it would be humanly impossible to tell you everything about the Holy Spirit. We are talking about the Spirit of God, who has a Divine constitution and such a superior mind it would be impossible to talk deeply about Him. But I can tell you about some things that are commonly known.

According to the Larger catechism God the Father, the Son and the Spirit are one. "(...) these three are one true, eternal God, the same in substance, equal in power and glory; although

distinguished by their personal properties."
(Westminster Larger Catechism – Public Domain)

It is easy to understand God the Father is our creator and sustainer, and Jesus, God the Son, is our savior and advocate, but what about the Holy Spirit? What part does He have in our lives?

When Jesus died on the cross, He reconnected us with God the Father. Our sins were forgiven, and God gave us a new chance. Jesus knew we were still in this world, and as long as we are here, we will still have a sinful nature.

How could we follow Jesus having a sinful nature? Who would remind us of what Jesus said when He was gone? Who would lead us to repentance when we fall? Who would transform our hearts? Who would teach us when Jesus was gone? That's why Jesus asked the Father to send His Spirit. Definitely, we would need a helper. So, Jesus promised the Spirit. God sent the Holy Spirit in Acts 2, so after this day, the Spirit started living inside our hearts to help us in our journey of faith.

The Bible says the Spirit sets us free and bears fruit in us. He helps us to follow the Lord's decrees and keep God's laws. He washes us and renews us, He is our comforter, and He is the one who teaches us all things, bringing all things to remembrance.

Remember the day you wanted to say something to a person in need and the verse of the Bible just popped up in your mind? It was the Holy Spirit. Or the day you were down and suddenly, out of nowhere, there is this verse of the Bible or a teaching of Jesus in your mind, which helped you to feel better? It was the Holy Spirit. And the list goes on and on.

All this introduction is to get to this point. In the end times, listening to the Holy Spirit will be essential because there will be many voices around us, and many of those won't come from the Lord. False prophets will multiply in the end times. They will be charming and convincing, but their teachings will be far away from the Word of God.

They will tell you, "Don't worry, Jesus is not coming now. Relax. You don't have to be ready.

You don't have to confess. You don't have to repent. You're fine. You are good to go." It happened the same in the book of Jeremiah. The prophet knew God would bring judgment over Israel. He told people to repent, but the false prophets told people this was not the case at all. According to them, Jeremiah was too negative, that was not happening. Who would you rather be listening to? A prophet telling God is bringing judgment or one telling you are going to be prosperous? You know who they decided to listen to, right? And there was nothing Jeremiah could do.

The Spirit of God is called the "Spirit of Truth." You can trust in Him. If He is telling you Jesus is coming, get ready because He is. According to John 16: 13, He is our guide. There are many voices in this world, some of them are Godly, but some of them are not. The Holy Spirit is the one who will guide you. He will tell you where to go, what to say and what to do. But for us to listen to the voice of the Spirit, we need to be connected with God. We need to open our hearts to the Lord and seek a close relationship with Him. If you are deeply connected with the Lord, the Spirit will guide you.

**

More verses about the Spirit: Rm 15:13, 1 Co 6: 19-20, John 14:16, Ezequiel 36:27, John 15:26, Titus 3:5, John 16:7, John 14: 26.

4. Sing a New Song to the Lord

Whenever you read the book of Revelation you realize how important worship in Heaven is. In Chapter 4:8-11, for example, the four living creatures and the twenty-four elders worship God the Father with their words.

In Revelation 5: 8-13, Jesus is worshipped as the Lamb of God by the twenty-four elders, as they sing to the Lord Jesus a new song. The angels, thousands of them, every creature on Earth, in Heaven, under the Earth and under the sea speak words of praise to Jesus.

In Revelation 7: 9-11, The Great Multitude from every nation, people, tribe, and language cried in a loud voice, "Salvation belongs to our God, who sits on the throne, and to the Lamb." Worshiping both God the Father and Jesus.

What does worship mean? Why is worship so important and so present in Heaven? Why is worship a tool in our Christian journey? Worship is "The act of paying divine honors to the Supreme Being; religious reverence and homage; adoration, or acts of reverence, paid to God, or a being viewed as God." (Webster's, 1913)

So when we worship God, we are in fact recognizing how great He is. We are recognizing He is infinitely bigger and is a far superior power than we are.

Praising, on the other hand, is "The joyful tribute of gratitude or homage rendered to the Divine Being; the act of glorifying or extolling the Creator; worship, particularly worship by song (...)" (Webster's, 1913)

When we are praising God, we are expressing our admiration and gratitude towards Him, for who He is and for what He is doing in our lives. It is something warm, passionate and it reflects all the fondness we have for God.

Some people mistakenly think praising or worshipping God is just a bunch of feel-good music you sing to feel better while you are in the church, but that's far from the truth. There is something powerful and supernatural in worshiping which many people haven't experienced yet.

When we pray, we talk to God. When we read the Bible, God talks to us, but when we worship, we connect to God in a beautiful way. It is like the divine and humankind are having an encounter and powerful things come from it.

God wants us to humble ourselves as servants before Him. At the same time we recognize His greatness, love, and the wonderful things He has done for us. But God is also our Heavenly Father, and as a Father He eagerly desires to connect with us.

Taking a moment to worship God is like a moment we have with someone we deeply love. We hug the person, look in the person's eyes in a warm and confident way and say "I love you. Thank you for all you've done for me."

If you have had a moment like this with someone, you know what I am talking about. A moment of deep connection which fills our cups.

This is worship. This is praise. From these moments of intimacy, of humbling and gratitude, comes the joy in being connected and closer to the One who created us and loves us with a perfect love.

Paul and Silas connected with God in such a powerful way when they were in jail. They were praying and singing to the Lord in such a deep way the doors of their cell opened, and they were so full of God's presence they didn't leave the jail, His magnificent presence in that place was enough for them.

The closer we are to Jesus' return, the more this world will be chaotic and even more troubled, but the peace, the joy, the comfort, and the overflowing love we can find in the Lord when we worship, will help us to face the challenges on our way.

Keep worshiping. Keep praising. Amazing things happen when we pour out our hearts before the Lord.

5. Time to Serve

It is impossible to talk about Christianity without speaking of service. That's why I chose *service* to be inserted in this block of chapters. Christianity and service are closely connected, they simply go together.

The love of God for humanity is the foundation of Christianity, and the love of someone without action is not real love. Jesus proved this when He was in this world, His arrival itself was one of the biggest proofs of love and service. When God the Father, the Creator, the Sustainer of this world decided to send His son to save us, He proved how much He loved us. Jesus, His son, would be away from home for over thirty years, confined in a human and limited body only to rescue us.

Jesus submitting Himself to leave His glorious body was His biggest proof of His perfect love to the Father and to us. As written in John 15:13, He dedicated himself to serve, and give His life for others.

The Holy Spirit expressed His love for us when He accepted to live in our hearts, in our imperfect, broken and sinful hearts and to help us to change what we couldn't change in ourselves. The three of them loved us, served us and continue to do so every single day under the sun.

The kingdom of God is made of love and service, and He expects us to do the same (I John 3:18). Jesus held serving others to such a high standard He said to the disciples in Mark 10:44-45, "Whoever wants to be first must be slave of all. For even the Son of Man did not come to be served, but to serve, and to give His life as a ransom for many."

The Christian church was created by Jesus and started with twelve servants who chose to leave their lives behind to follow Him. They also dedicated their lives to love and serve God and people. During their ministries, they served, loved, healed, helped and shared the hope of the gospel with others and helped them to grow spiritually.

Throughout human history, I can't think of a single time where the church hasn't impacted the community around it. Every movie I watch about the Second World War, for example, has at least the Salvation Army feeding the hungry, and helping others with their needs.

The end times will be a time of anguish and desperation. A time when everything we have known as normal or regular until that point, won't be the same anymore. These constant changes, uncertainties, and the spread of evil will lead people to act in desperation. Once again, the church will be needed as an agent of Christ's love in this world.

When we think about the possibility of Jesus' return being closer, we may feel insecure. Are we going to be able to serve and love as the Apostles did in the past? Are we going to dedicate ourselves to the kingdom as others did before us? Scriptures are proof God uses imperfect people to do His amazing work.

God does not make mistakes. If you are here in a time of uncertainty, it is because you have to be here. It is not by accident. We will be the ones who will comfort people in times of pain, loss and suffering until the Scriptures are fulfilled.

Once again in human history, the church will be invited to serve, help and bless people in all sorts of ways. No gift can be wasted. If the Lord gave you the gift of cleaning, use it. If the Lord gave you the gift of teaching, use it. Every little act of love and compassion will be used as a proof of God's love for humankind.

Each one of us is sent to this world with a mission, and in the process of the end times, our mission is bigger than surviving it ourselves. Our mission is to be the servants of the Lord on this Earth until the Lord comes back for His church. Our mission is to be the ones who point to the cross which changed our lives forever.

Get ready. Get strong in the Lord. These troubled times shall pass, but in the end times we will be given a huge opportunity to serve and love others as Jesus wants us to do. Open your heart. Let Him prepare you to share His love with others, the same way someone did it for you one day.

Keep Your Eyes on The Prize

The New Jerusalem

While some women when pregnant feel great, others do not as their bodies change too much. Their level of energy drops to the floor. They are always sleepy and tired, and their brains seem not to be functioning properly. They have cravings they don't understand. They get sick with some particular smells or tastes. They may even stop liking a certain type of food they have always loved, and the list goes on.

It usually gets worse in the end. Their feet become swollen and they can't get rid of that stubborn heartburn. It is hard to breathe or find a good position to sleep, etc. Let's not mention the contractions and the labor. But the truth is the expecting mothers put up with all those things because they know what their reward will be, and they can't wait for it.

When they finally see their babies, all the hardships will be forgotten. They won't remember about the heartburn, the sleepless nights, or the lack of energy. All the pain and suffering will be replaced by the joy found in motherhood.

We can make the same parallel between the end of the world and *The New Jerusalem*. The same way keeping our eyes on the prize helps us to be resilient during pregnancy, the promise of the New Jerusalem helps endure the hardships set to happen in the last days.

But what does the Bible say about the New Jerusalem?

After justice happened on Earth against all evil, John writes in Revelation 21 what he saw. He saw a new Heaven and Earth. He saw the New Jerusalem coming down from heaven, prepared as a bride and waiting for her groom. In this city, the glory of God was shining, and it shone like a precious jewel. The city had twelve gates on which were written the names of the twelve tribes of Israel, and it had twelve foundations, named after the twelve Apostles of Jesus.

On a side note, I absolutely love the last part because the twelve doors are a clear reference of the alliance the Lord made with those who believed Him in the Old Testament. The twelve foundations are a reference of the alliance the Lord made with those who believed Him in the New Testament, connecting both testaments in a beautiful way. The new and the old covenants are present in the New Jerusalem.

The city is made with the finest precious jewels and there is not a temple because God and Jesus themselves were their temple. There is no need for a sun or moon because God and the Lamb are their light.

There is a river flowing from God and Jesus' throne, this river is called the River of the Water of Life. The Tree of Life was on each side of the river, yielding fruit all year around. Its leaves have healing properties. There will be no more curses. And they shall reign forever.

In Revelation 21:5, the Lord says He is making everything new. At that point, His work was finished. For He is the Alpha and Omega, the Beginning and End. Those who are victorious (who persevere in faith) will inherit it all. Jesus will be their God and they will be His children.

Isaiah 35 also talks about the New Jerusalem. He talks in a beautiful and poetic way about the joy of the redeemed ones. He said the blind will see, the deaf will hear, the mute will shout with joy, and those with mobility issues will leap. We will be completely redeemed. The unclean won't be there, only those who were redeemed by the Lord.

Wouldn't you like to exchange this troubled and broken place for this new one? I guess we all would. Peace at last. Forever.

The blood of Christ, our faith in Him. His grace upon us. His Spirit working in us. Seeking a true and a deep relationship with the Lord is what will lead us to our forever home. We believe in His promises. We believe He is really preparing this place of Eternal peace for us, where we can join the Spirit and say "Come." "Lord Jesus, come!"

***

"Strengthen the feeble hands, steady the knees that give way; say to those with fearful hearts, be strong, do not fear, your God will come, He will come with vengeance; with divine retribution. He will come to save you." Isaiah 35: 3 and 4.

Be Prepared

– Put Your House in Order

Writing this book was as challenging as I thought it would be. By the grace of God, we did it, and we hope some of it has remained in your heart, in order to inspire and strengthen you in the tough days ahead.

Here are some of the things we've talked about in this book. In the last days, love will grow cold, people will be unloving and unkind. However, Jesus still invites us to stay firm in His love, loving Him and our neighbors, at the same time we protect our hearts.

We've learned that Jesus sees and acknowledges what we do for Him and His kingdom. He wants us to seek Him, to grow in faith, to repent from our sins and to be committed to His kingdom and His Word. Ultimately, He has the most beautiful promises to those who are to be found faithful to the end.

We learned Jesus doesn't want us to navigate the tough days in the dark. He has given us a lot of information about what is set to happen. It is all in the Bible, all the signs which are to be witnessed. All we have to do is to seek, learn and study about it.

Listening to the Holy Spirit in the last days is going to be essential to our survival. He is the One who will give us the right direction, in the midst of all the other voices (false prophets, rumors, etc.). He is the one who will tell us the right way to go.

We learned even when we see evil spread in this world, our prayers can still be heard and answered in a favorable way. For the Lord we serve and love, it is powerful and has authority over any problem, hardship, or disease.

We learned taking a deep breath, worshiping, reading the Bible, or keeping ourselves busy may help us to cope in the tough days.

Ultimately, we learned that keeping our eyes on the prize, the New Jerusalem, our forever home, will give us hope to keep going in times of trouble.

We pray this book has blessed you to discover new things or remember some of the teachings we find in the Bible.

Thank you for running this race with us,

Blessings,

Dea A. Myers

Other Titles from the Author

HOPE (We All Need It)

The Book of the Secrets – Book 1 – Novel

Never an Accident

Faith in the Season

My Prayer Requests Book

2-in-1 Dea A. Myers Book Collection

All titles available at www.deaamyers.com

About the Author

Dea A. Myers is a Christian author who is passionate to positively inspire people. She is the author of the inspirational, "HOPE-We All Need It," released in 2020. Her first novel, "The Book of the Secrets - Book I," was published in 2021. Dea A. Myers is also passionate about many forms of arts, as seen by her holiday book "Faith in the Season," also released in 2021. In 2022, Myers published "Never an Accident," and "My Prayer Requests Book," as well as "2-in-1 Dea A. Myers' Book Collection." The author now releases in 2023 a new inspirational book called "Encouragement for the End Times." Myers lives in Georgia with her husband and children.

NOTES